United States Government Accountability Office

Report to Congressional Committees

I044860 4

November 2013

HURRICANE SANDY RELIEF

Improved Guidance on Designing Internal Control Plans Could Enhance Oversight of Disaster Funding

November 2013

GAO Highlights

Highlights of GAO-14-58, a report to congressional committees

HURRICANE SANDY RELIEF

Improved Guidance on Designing Internal Control Plans Could Enhance Oversight of Disaster Funding

Why GAO Did This Study

In late October 2012, Hurricane Sandy devastated portions of the Mid-Atlantic and northeastern United States, leaving victims of the storm and their communities in need of financial assistance for disaster relief aid. On January 29, 2013, the President signed the Disaster Relief Appropriations Act, 2013, which provided approximately $50 billion in supplemental appropriations, before sequestration, to 61 programs at 19 federal agencies for expenses related to the consequences of Hurricane Sandy. The act required agencies to submit internal control plans for the funds in accordance with OMB criteria by March 31, 2013.

The act mandated GAO to review the design of agencies' internal control plans. This report addresses the extent to which (1) the internal control plans prepared by federal agencies complied with OMB guidance and (2) OMB's guidance was effective for providing comprehensive oversight of the internal control risks for the programs receiving funds for Sandy disaster relief. To address these objectives, GAO reviewed agencies' Sandy disaster relief internal control plans; M-13-07; and relevant GAO, inspector general, and financial statement audit reports. GAO also reviewed the internal control plans and M-13-07 against internal control standards.

What GAO Recommends

GAO recommends that OMB develop more robust guidance for agencies to design internal control plans for future disaster relief funding. OMB staff generally agreed with GAO's recommendation.

View GAO-14-58. For more information, contact Beryl H. Davis at (202) 512-2623 or davisbh@gao.gov.

What GAO Found

In response to the Disaster Relief Appropriations Act, 2013, agencies prepared Hurricane Sandy disaster relief internal control plans based on Office of Management and Budget (OMB) guidance but did not consistently apply the guidance in preparing these plans. OMB Memorandum M-13-07 (M-13-07), *Accountability for Funds Provided by the Disaster Relief Appropriations Act*, directed federal agencies to provide a description of incremental risks they identified for Sandy disaster relief funding as well as an internal control strategy for mitigating these risks. Each of the 19 agencies responsible for the 61 programs receiving funds under the act submitted an internal control plan with specific program details using a template provided by OMB. Agencies' plans ranged from providing most of the required information to not providing any information on certain programs. For example, each of the 61 programs was required to discuss its protocol for improper payments; however, GAO found that 38 programs included this information, 11 included partial information, and 12 included no information.

OMB's guidance was an important step in the oversight of Sandy disaster funding, addressing internal controls, improper payments protocol, and unexpended grant funds. However, several weaknesses limited its effectiveness in providing a comprehensive oversight mechanism for these funds. Specifically, the guidance (1) focused on the identification of incremental risks without adequate linkages to demonstrate that known risks had been adequately addressed, (2) provided agencies with significant flexibility without requirements for documentation or criteria for claiming exceptions, and (3) resulted in certain agencies developing their internal control plans at the same time that funds needed to be quickly distributed. GAO found that OMB guidance:

- Asked agencies to focus on mitigating incremental risk, so the resulting plans did not provide comprehensive information on all known risks and internal controls that may affect the programs that received funding. Linking the additional risks identified in the plans to the complete set of known risks and related internal controls can help agency management and Congress to provide effective oversight of the funds.

- Allowed agencies significant flexibility in deciding whether they needed to design additional internal controls, and did not provide specific criteria for agencies to claim exemptions from requirements. GAO found that some agencies did not discuss certain additional internal controls in their plans, despite having identified incremental risks.

- Did not require agencies to document their rationales for not including additional internal controls in their plans. As a result, it was not apparent from the internal control plans the extent to which the agencies considered the need for these additional internal controls.

- Was developed and issued in a short time frame in response to the act. By the time that the agencies submitted their internal control plans on March 31, 2013, they reported that they had already obligated approximately $4.6 billion. Standard internal control guidance for disaster funding could help ensure that controls are designed timely.

_____ United States Government Accountability Office

Contents

Figures

Abbreviations

DHS	Department of Homeland Security
DOC	Department of Commerce
DOD	Department of Defense
DOI	Department of the Interior
DOJ	Department of Justice
DOL	Department of Labor
DOT	Department of Transportation
EPA	Environmental Protection Agency
GSA	General Services Administration
HHS	Department of Health and Human Services
HUD	Department of Housing and Urban Development
IG	inspector general
LSC	Legal Services Corporation
NASA	National Aeronautics and Space Administration
NDRF	National Disaster Recovery Framework
OMB	Office of Management and Budget
SBA	Small Business Administration
SSA	Social Security Administration
USACE	U.S. Army Corps of Engineers
USDA	Department of Agriculture
VA	Department of Veterans Affairs

GAO   U.S. GOVERNMENT ACCOUNTABILITY OFFICE

441 G St. N.W.
Washington, DC 20548

November 26, 2013

The Honorable Barbara A. Mikulski
Chairwoman
The Honorable Richard C. Shelby
Vice Chairman
Committee on Appropriations
United States Senate

The Honorable Harold Rogers
Chairman
The Honorable Nita M. Lowey
Ranking Member
Committee on Appropriations
House of Representatives

In late October 2012, Hurricane Sandy devastated portions of the Mid-Atlantic and northeastern United States, leaving victims of the storm and their communities in need of immediate disaster relief aid. On January 29, 2013, the President signed the Disaster Relief Appropriations Act, 2013 (Disaster Relief Act),[1] which included approximately $50 billion in supplemental appropriations for fiscal year 2013 to 61 specific programs or appropriation accounts at 19 federal agencies for expenses related to the consequences of Hurricane Sandy.[2] The Disaster Relief Act required these federal agencies to submit their plans for ensuring internal control over the Sandy disaster relief funding by March 31, 2013, to GAO, respective inspectors general (IG), the Office of Management and Budget (OMB), and the Committees on Appropriations of the U.S. Senate and the House of Representatives.

The Disaster Relief Act also required OMB to establish criteria for the agencies to follow in developing internal control plans for managing the risks associated with the additional Sandy disaster-related funding. On March 12, 2013, OMB established these criteria in Memorandum M-13-07 (M-13-07), *Accountability for Funds Provided by the Disaster Relief*

---

[1]Pub. L. No. 113-2, div. A, 127 Stat. 4 (Jan. 29, 2013).

[2]In this report, we use "programs" to refer to the programs or appropriation accounts for which agencies received funds under the Disaster Relief Act.

Appropriations Act.[3] The Disaster Relief Act mandated GAO to review the design of the internal control plans for each federal agency receiving funds. In response to the mandate, on June 28, 2013, we briefed your committee staffs on our preliminary observations and discussed the extent to which federal agencies designed effective internal control plans for their programs that received funds for Sandy disaster relief.

This report provides the results of our final review to determine the extent to which (1) the internal control plans prepared by federal agencies complied with OMB guidance and (2) OMB's guidance was effective for providing comprehensive oversight of the internal control risks for the programs receiving funds for Sandy disaster relief. To address our objectives, we reviewed the Sandy disaster relief internal control plans for the 19 federal agencies administering the 61 programs receiving funds under the Disaster Relief Act and compared them to M-13-07.[4] We reviewed the internal control plans and M-13-07 against *Standards for Internal Control in the Federal Government*.[5] In addition, we compared the agencies' identified incremental risks to prior GAO and IG findings associated with internal control risks for agency programs receiving funds for Sandy disaster relief.

We conducted this performance audit from March 2013 to November 2013 in accordance with generally accepted government auditing standards. Those standards require that we plan and perform the audit to obtain sufficient, appropriate evidence to provide a reasonable basis for our findings and conclusions based on our audit objectives. We believe that the evidence obtained provides a reasonable basis for our findings and conclusions based on our audit objectives. A more detailed explanation of our objectives, scope, and methodology can be found in appendix I.

---

[3]Office of Management and Budget, *Accountability for Funds Provided by the Disaster Relief Appropriations Act*, Memorandum No. M-13-07 (Mar. 12, 2013).

[4]In addition to other Department of Defense (DOD) components, Department of the Army—Army Corps of Engineers—Civil (USACE), received supplemental appropriations. For the purposes of this report, we treated USACE as one of the 19 federal agencies, separate from DOD.

[5]GAO, *Standards for Internal Control in the Federal Government*, GAO/AIMD-00-21.3.1 (Washington, D.C.: November 1999), provides an overall framework for establishing and maintaining internal control and for identifying and addressing major performance and management challenges and areas at greatest risk of fraud, waste and abuse, and mismanagement.

Background

Disaster Relief Act

The Disaster Relief Act included approximately $50 billion in supplemental appropriations for fiscal year 2013 to 19 agencies for 61 specific programs for expenses related to the consequences of Hurricane Sandy. Under the authority granted by the Balanced Budget and Emergency Deficit Control Act of 1985, as amended, OMB determined that these supplemental appropriations were to be included in the fiscal year 2013 base subject to sequestration under section 251A of that act.[6] The amounts included in this report are drawn from the Disaster Relief Act as originally enacted, and are not adjusted to account for sequestration.[7] Figure 1 shows the distribution of Sandy disaster relief funding by agency. Appendix II presents more detailed information on the supplemental appropriations provided by the Disaster Relief Act.

---

[6]2 U.S.C. § 901a. *See also* Office of Management and Budget, *OMB Report to the Congress on the Joint Committee Sequestration for Fiscal Year 2013* (Mar. 1, 2013) (*OMB Sequestration Report*), and GAO, *March 1 Joint Committee Sequestration for Fiscal Year 2013*, B-324723 (Washington, D.C.: July 31, 2013).

[7]The majority of appropriation accounts that received funding under the Disaster Relief Act were categorized as nondefense discretionary spending and therefore were subject to a reduction of 5.0 percent of their budgetary resources. Accounts that were categorized as nondefense mandatory spending were subject to a 5.1 percent reduction, and accounts that were categorized as defense discretionary spending were subject to a 7.8 percent reduction. Some accounts were exempt from sequestration as well. The actual sequestration of Disaster Relief Act funds in a program, project, or activity within an account may vary, depending on other sources of sequestrable funding in the program. *See* Office of Management and Budget, *OMB Sequestration Report*.

Figure 1: Distribution of Appropriations Provided by the Disaster Relief Act

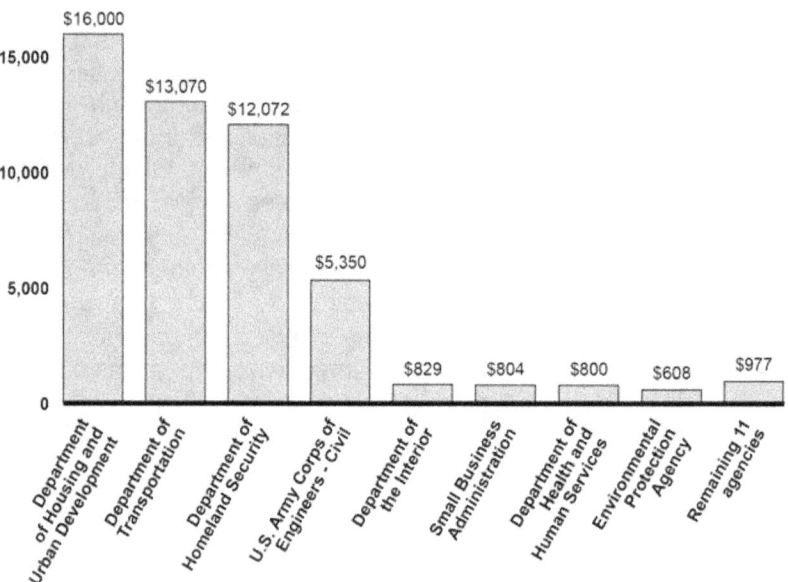

Source: GAO analysis of the Disaster Relief Appropriations Act, 2013

Note: Amounts do not reflect reductions based on subsequent sequestration.

Most of the agencies' supplemental appropriations provided by the Disaster Relief Act are related to grant programs. As shown in figure 2, grant programs received more than $41 billion of the approximately $50 billion provided by the Disaster Relief Act.

GAO-14-58 Hurricane Sandy Relief

Figure 2: Primary Type of Expenditures Authorized for Programs Funded under the Disaster Relief Act

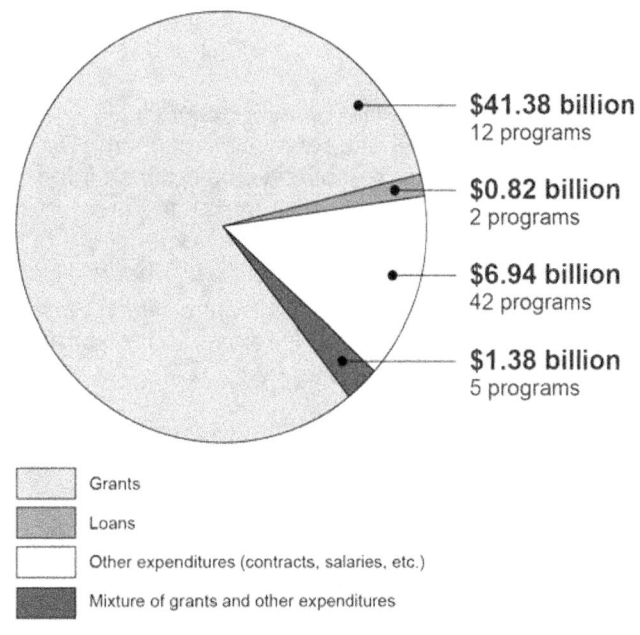

$41.38 billion
12 programs

$0.82 billion
2 programs

$6.94 billion
42 programs

$1.38 billion
5 programs

Grants

Loans

Other expenditures (contracts, salaries, etc.)

Mixture of grants and other expenditures

Source: GAO analysis of agencies' Sandy disaster relief internal control plans and the Disaster Relief Appropriations Act, 2013.

Note: Amounts do not reflect reductions based on subsequent sequestration.

The Disaster Relief Act also provides an oversight framework for these funds in regard to improper payments and the recapture of unexpended grant funds. Specifically, the Disaster Relief Act states that

- all programs and activities receiving these funds shall be deemed "susceptible to significant improper payments," for purposes of the Improper Payments Information Act of 2002 (IPIA),[8] and

- funds for grants shall be expended by the grantees within the 24-month period following the agency's obligation of funds for the grant, unless OMB waives this requirement for a particular grant program

---

[8]IPIA, as amended, requires agencies to annually develop a statistically valid estimate of improper payments for each program or activity "that may be susceptible to significant improper payments." See Pub. L. No. 107-300 (Nov. 26, 2002), *codified, as amended, at* 31 U.S.C. § 3321 note.

GAO-14-58 Hurricane Sandy Relief

and submits a written justification for such waiver to the Committees on Appropriations of the U.S. Senate and the House of Representatives. The act states that agencies shall include a term in the grant that requires the grantee to return any funds to the agency that are not expended within this 24-month period.

In addition, the Disaster Relief Act states that through September 30, 2015, the Recovery Accountability and Transparency Board (Recovery Board) shall develop and use information technology resources and oversight mechanisms to detect and remediate waste, fraud, and abuse in the obligation and expenditure of funds to support oversight of Sandy disaster relief funding.[9] The act also states that the Recovery Board will coordinate its activities with OMB, each federal agency receiving appropriations related to the impact of Hurricane Sandy, and the IG of each such agency.

OMB Guidance

As noted above, the Disaster Relief Act required OMB to establish criteria for agencies to use in developing their Sandy disaster relief internal control plans. Internal controls serve as the first line of defense in safeguarding assets and in preventing and detecting fraud, abuse, and errors. Given the magnitude of funding provided by the Disaster Relief Act, it is important for federal agencies to ensure that the funds appropriated under the act are used for their intended purposes. OMB established the criteria in M-13-07, which provides an overview of the internal control planning and reporting requirements for all programs funded under the act with a focus on (1) developing additional internal controls warranted beyond previously existing controls, (2) managing all Sandy disaster-related funding with the same discipline and rigor as programs that are traditionally designated as high risk for improper payments, and (3) managing unexpended grant funds. M-13-07 notes that as required by OMB Circular No. A-123, *Management's Responsibility for Internal Control* (OMB Circular A-123), agencies must have established internal control plans to prevent waste, fraud, and abuse

---

[9]The Recovery Board is a nonpartisan, nonpolitical agency created by the American Recovery and Reinvestment Act of 2009 (Recovery Act). The goals of the Recovery Board are to provide transparency of Recovery Act-related funds and to detect and prevent fraud, waste, and mismanagement. The board currently consists of 12 IGs. While the Recovery Board's Recovery Act-related activities were supposed to end on September 30, 2013, the Disaster Relief Act requires that the Recovery Board provide oversight of Hurricane Sandy funding through September 30, 2015.

of federal program funds.[10] Specifically, OMB Circular A-123 states that management is responsible for establishing and maintaining internal control to achieve the objectives of effective and efficient operations, reliable financial reporting, and compliance with applicable laws and regulations.

As illustrated in figure 3, OMB directed agencies to describe incremental risks identified for each program administering Sandy disaster relief funding as well as the internal control strategy for mitigating each of these risks (if applicable).

---

[10]Office of Management and Budget, *Management's Responsibility for Internal Control*, Circular No. A-123 (Washington, D.C.: Dec. 21, 2004).

Figure 3: Sandy Disaster Relief Internal Control Plan Template Contained in OMB Memorandum M-13-07

ATTACHMENT
Sandy Relief Internal Control Plan

Date:

Agency:

Please submit one internal control plan for the agency as a whole with program details provided in the table below.

Using the table below, describe the incremental risks identified with each program administering Sandy recovery funding as well as the internal control strategy (specific policies and procedures enhancements) for mitigating each of these risks. Note that the risk assessment should reflect the agency strategy on reducing improper payments, promoting effective grants management, and ensuring the integrity of acquisitions. Further, the plans should address efforts to conduct additional levels of review, increase monitoring and oversight of grant recipients, enhance collaboration with the inspector general community, expedite review and resolution of audit findings, and adopt improper payments management protocol.

Program Name	Funded Activities	Risks Associated with Funded Activities	Mitigation Strategy
Program Name	Provide a brief description of the actions being taken by the program in response to Sandy.	Provide a description of incremental risks[6] associated with the actions being taken in response to Sandy.	Provide a description of actions being taken to address the increased risk identified, including governance structure, policies and procedures, communication strategies, and monitoring and oversight mechanisms.

---

[6] If incremental risks are not identified, management can also describe how risks are accepted and managed as part of ongoing monitoring activities.

Source: OMB Memorandum M-13-07.

M-13-07 also discusses the roles of other parties involved in supporting Sandy disaster relief efforts, including the Recovery Board, the Hurricane Sandy Rebuilding Task Force (Task Force), and agency IGs. The Task Force was established on December 7, 2012, under Executive Order

13632.[11] M-13-07 states that the Task Force is responsible for identifying opportunities for federal agencies to work together to support recovery from Hurricane Sandy and to promote strong accountability for the use of the disaster relief funds. M-13-07 also notes that the Task Force is supported by a program management office that is working with agencies to ensure stakeholder engagement, establish performance metrics to gauge recovery efforts, and monitor the execution of Sandy disaster relief funding. Further, M-13-07 emphasizes that agency internal control plans should reflect consideration of early and frequent engagement between agencies and IGs to discuss issues affecting the Disaster Relief Act's disaster-related programs and activities in order to identify and mitigate potential risk.

In addition to issuing M-13-07, OMB took steps to help agencies develop internal control plans for managing the risks related to Sandy funds. These activities occurred prior to and following the release of the guidance. On February 19, 2013, OMB sent the Chief Financial Officer community advance notice of the forthcoming OMB guidance. This notice identified minimum requirements for agency internal control plans that would be included and further explained in the OMB guidance. Also, as reported by OMB staff and agency officials, OMB met with the agencies to discuss agency risk assessments and the development of internal control plans.

Agencies Did Not Consistently Apply OMB M-13-07 in Preparing Their Sandy Disaster Relief Internal Control Plans

In accordance with M-13-07, each of the 19 agencies that received funds under the act submitted a Sandy disaster relief internal control plan with specific program details using the template provided by OMB. OMB guidance directed agencies to develop internal control plans based on incremental risk. We found that agencies identified incremental risk related to Sandy activities for 38 of the 61 programs receiving funding under the Disaster Relief Act. Our review of the internal control plans disclosed that agencies did not consistently apply M-13-07 in preparing these plans. Specifically, agencies' plans ranged from providing most of the required information to not providing any information on certain

---

[11]The Executive Order states that in collaboration with the leadership provided through the National Disaster Recovery Framework (NDRF), the Task Force will identify opportunities for achieving rebuilding success, consistent with the NDRF's commitment to support economic vitality, enhance public health and safety, protect and enhance natural and manmade infrastructure, and ensure appropriate accountability. See Exec. Order No. 13632, *Establishing the Hurricane Sandy Rebuilding Task Force*, 77 Fed. Reg. 74,341 (Dec. 14, 2012).

programs. M-13-07 provides an overview of the internal control planning and reporting requirements for all programs funded under the act with a focus on three major areas: (1) additional internal controls for Sandy-related activities, (2) improper payments protocol, and (3) management of unexpended grant funds.

Additional Internal Controls for Sandy-Related Activities

M-13-07 states that agency internal control plans for Sandy-related program funding shall reflect consideration of elements such as conducting additional levels of review, increasing monitoring and oversight of grant recipients, continuing collaboration with the IG community, and expediting review and resolution of audit findings.

Conducting Additional Levels of Review

The first element of additional internal control listed in M-13-07 is additional levels of review of award decisions, payment transactions, and other critical process elements that impact the use of Disaster Relief Act funds. This requirement applied to the 38 programs that identified incremental risk related to Sandy disaster relief funding. However, M-13-07 notes that agencies should adopt more expansive review procedures, as appropriate. This allowed agencies to determine whether additional levels of review were necessary for their award decisions, payment transactions, and other critical process elements. M-13-07 did not require agencies to document their rationales for determining whether additional levels of review were appropriate. Table 1 summarizes the requirement to conduct additional levels of review per M-13-07.

Table 1: Conducting Additional Levels of Review per M-13-07

Requirement: Agencies shall adopt more expansive review procedures, as appropriate, to scrutinize the following items. To ensure a higher degree of accountability, each agency shall include senior-level officials in these reviews, as appropriate.		
Item for more expansive review	Required of	Exception to requirement
a. Award decisions.	Programs that identified incremental risk	Not required if agency determines it to not be appropriate
b. Payment transactions.		
c. Other critical process elements that impact the use of Disaster Relief Act funds.		

Source: GAO analysis of OMB Memorandum M-13-07.

As illustrated in table 2, our review found that agencies' discussion in their internal control plans of conducting additional levels of review for 38 programs that identified incremental risk related to Sandy activities varied. Certain agencies did not discuss additional levels of review for programs for which they identified incremental risk. Of the 38 programs that identified incremental risk, 8 programs did not discuss award decisions, 11 programs did not discuss payment transactions, and 12 programs did not discuss critical process elements that impact the use of Disaster Relief Act funds. However, it is not clear from the Sandy disaster relief internal control plans whether these agencies determined that additional levels of review were not appropriate for these programs.

While the requirement for additional levels of review did not apply to the 23 programs that did not identify incremental risk, some agencies also discussed conducting additional levels of review for certain programs for which they did not identify incremental risk in their Sandy disaster relief internal control plans. Of the 23 programs that did not identify incremental risk, 5 programs discussed additional levels of review for award decisions, payment transactions, and other critical process elements. For example, one agency planned to add an additional level of review by establishing an executive council to make final decisions on project selection for its Hurricane Sandy funding.

Table 2: Discussion of Conducting Additional Levels of Review in Agencies' Sandy Disaster Relief Internal Control Plans

The agency's internal control plan discusses conducting additional levels of review, including more expansive review and review by senior-level officials, as appropriate, for	Number of programs					
	Identified incremental risk	Did not identify incremental risk	Total	Yes	Partial[a]	No
a. Award decisions.	38	5	**43**	18	17	8
b. Payment transactions.	38	5	**43**	13	19	11
c. Other critical process elements that impact the use of Disaster Relief Act funds.	38	5	**43**	21	10	12

Source: GAO analysis of agencies' Sandy disaster relief internal control plans.

[a]A "partial" response indicates that the agency described an existing, not additional, review process to satisfy the intent of the requirement.

Increasing Monitoring and Oversight of Grant Recipients

The second element of additional internal control listed in M-13-07 is increasing monitoring and oversight of grant recipients through (1) increased frequency and specificity of grantee reports, (2) additional site visits, and (3) additional technical assistance and training for grant recipients. This requirement applies to all 17 grant programs that identified incremental risk related to Sandy disaster relief funding. However, M-13-07 notes that agencies should adopt increased monitoring and oversight of grant recipients to the extent appropriate and possible under budgetary constraints. This allowed agencies to justify not designing controls for increased monitoring and oversight of grant recipients because of low program risk or budgetary constraints. M-13-07 did not require agencies to document their rationales for determining whether increased monitoring and oversight of grant recipients were appropriate. Table 3 summarizes the requirement to increase monitoring and oversight of grant recipients per M-13-07.

Table 3: Increasing Monitoring and Oversight of Grant Recipients per M-13-07

Requirement: To the extent appropriate to mitigate risk and possible under budgetary constraints, agencies shall increase the following monitoring and oversight mechanisms for grant recipients.

Monitoring and oversight mechanisms	Required of	Exception to requirement
a. Increased frequency and specificity of grantee reporting.	Grant programs that identified incremental risk	Not required if agency determines it to not be appropriate or possible under budgetary constraints
b. Additional site visits.		
c. Additional technical assistance and training for grant recipients.		

Source: GAO analysis of OMB Memorandum M-13-07.

As illustrated in table 4, our review found that agencies' discussion in their internal control plans of increasing monitoring and oversight of grant recipients varied. For most of the 17 grant programs, agencies planned to increase monitoring and oversight mechanisms for their grant recipients. For example, one agency planned to increase monitoring and oversight of grant recipients by requiring financial and milestone progress reports from its Hurricane Sandy grantees on a monthly basis, rather than quarterly, as required of its other grantees.

Conversely, certain agencies did not discuss additional monitoring and oversight of grant recipients for some grant programs. Specifically, of the 17 grant programs, 5 did not discuss increasing the frequency and specificity of grantee reporting, 6 did not discuss conducting additional site visits, and 9 did not discuss providing additional technical assistance and training to recipients. However, it is not clear from the Sandy disaster relief internal control plans whether these agencies determined that increasing monitoring and oversight of grant recipients was not necessary for these programs or not possible under budgetary constraints.

GAO-14-58 Hurricane Sandy Relief

Table 4: Discussion of Increasing Monitoring and Oversight of Grant Recipients in Agencies' Sandy Disaster Relief Internal Control Plans

The agency's internal control plan discusses increased monitoring and oversight of grant recipients, to the extent appropriate and possible under budgetary constraints, through	Number of programs			
	Total	Yes	Partial[a]	No
a. Increased frequency and specificity of grantee reporting.	17	11	1	5
b. Conducting additional site visits.	17	9	2	6
c. Providing additional technical assistance and training to recipients.	17	8	0	9

Source: GAO analysis of agencies' Sandy disaster relief internal control plans.

[a]A "partial" response indicates that the agency described an existing, not additional, mechanism for grantee oversight to satisfy the intent of the requirement.

Continuing Collaboration with the Inspector General Community

The third element of additional internal control listed in M-13-07 is that agencies should continue early and frequent engagement with their respective IG. This requirement applied to all programs that identified incremental risk related to Sandy disaster relief funding. Table 5 summarizes the requirement to collaborate with the IG community per M-13-07.

Table 5: Continuing Collaboration with the Inspector General Community per M-13-07

Requirement	Required of	Exception to requirement
To identify and mitigate potential risk, agencies shall continue early and frequent engagement with inspectors general to discuss issues affecting the Disaster Relief Act's disaster-related programs and activities.	Programs that identified incremental risk	No exception

Source: GAO analysis of OMB Memorandum M-13-07.

As illustrated in table 6, our review found that agencies discussed collaboration with their IGs for most programs, regardless of whether they identified incremental risk. For example, one agency noted in its Sandy disaster relief internal control plan that it planned to hold monthly meetings with its IG to discuss ongoing audits and foster additional coordination through participation in program conferences and training. While the requirement for continued collaboration with the IG community applied to the 38 programs that identified incremental risk, 15 programs that did not identify incremental risk also discussed continuing collaboration with their respective IGs in their Sandy disaster relief internal control plans. Of the 38 programs that identified incremental risk, 3 did not discuss continuing collaboration with the agency's IG to identify and mitigate potential risk.

Table 6: Discussion of Continuing Collaboration with the Inspector General Community in Agencies' Sandy Disaster Relief Internal Control Plans

	Number of programs					
	Identified incremental risk	Did not identify incremental risk	Total	Yes	Partial[a]	No
The agency's internal control plan discusses continuing collaboration with the agency's IG to identify and mitigate potential risk.	38	15	**53**	45	5	3

Source: GAO analysis of agencies' Sandy disaster relief internal control plans.

[a]A "partial" response indicates that the agency described its process for general collaboration with the agency's IG but did not explain how this collaboration would involve Hurricane Sandy funding.

Expediting Review and Resolution of Audit Findings

The fourth element of additional internal control listed in M-13-07 is that agencies should expedite the review and resolution of audit findings. M-13-07 states that agencies shall resolve all audit findings, which include findings from GAO, IG, and single audit reports,[12] within 6 months after completion of the audit to the extent practicable. This requirement applied to all programs that identified incremental risk. Additionally, for grant programs that identified incremental risk, M-13-07 states that agencies should avoid granting extension requests for audit report submission and should explore the feasibility of conducting additional audit activities to review internal control procedures prior to funding the activity. Table 7 summarizes the requirement to expedite review and resolution of audit findings per M-13-07.

---

[12]The Single Audit Act, 31 U.S.C. §§ 7501-7507, requires states, local governments, and nonprofit entities expending $500,000 or more in federal financial assistance annually to undergo either an audit specific to the program under which they receive that assistance or a "single audit" covering the operations of the entire entity. Reports of these audits are conveyed to federal agencies via a government-wide clearinghouse.

Table 7: Expediting Review and Resolution of Audit Findings per M-13-07

Requirement	Required of	Exception to requirement
Agencies shall resolve all audit findings (GAO, IG, single audit) within 6 months after completion of the audit to the extent practicable.	Programs that identified incremental risk	Not required if agency determines it to not be practicable
Agencies should avoid granting extension requests for audit report submissions.	Grant programs that identified incremental risk	No exception
Agencies should explore the feasibility of conducting additional audit activities to review internal control procedures prior to funding the activity.	Grant programs that identified incremental risk	Not required if agency determines it to not be feasible

Source: GAO analysis of OMB Memorandum M-13-07.

As illustrated in table 8, our review found that agencies' discussion in their internal control plans of expediting review and resolution of audit findings varied. While the requirement applied to the 38 programs that identified incremental risk, not all agencies discussed resolving all audit findings within 6 months after completion of the audit. Specifically, of the 38 programs, there were 12 programs that identified incremental risk and did not discuss expediting review and resolution of audit findings in their internal control plans. However, while the requirement applied to the 38 programs that identified incremental risk, 5 programs that did not identify incremental risk also discussed expediting review and resolution of audit findings in their Sandy disaster relief internal control plans.

For the 17 grant programs, agencies did not discuss avoidance of granting extension requests for audit report submission and exploring the feasibility of conducting additional audit activities prior to funding the activity. Specifically, for the 17 grant programs, 14 did not discuss avoiding granting extension requests for audit report submission and 11 did not discuss exploring the feasibility of conducting additional audit activities prior to funding the activity. It is not clear from the Sandy disaster relief internal control plans whether agencies determined that these additional audit activities prior to funding the activity would not be feasible.

Table 8: Discussion of Expediting Review and Resolution of Audit Findings in Agencies' Sandy Disaster Relief Internal Control Plans

The agency's internal control plan discusses the following related to expediting review and resolution of audit findings:	Number of programs					
	Identified incremental risk	Did not identify incremental risk	Total	Yes	Partial	No
a. Resolving all audit findings (GAO, IG, and single audit) within 6 months after completion of the audit to the extent practicable.	38	5	**43**	22	9[a]	12
b. Avoiding granting extension requests for audit report submissions.	17	0	**17**	2	1[b]	14
c. Exploring the feasibility of conducting additional audit activities to review internal control procedures prior to funding the activity.	17	0	**17**	1	5[c]	11

Source: GAO analysis of agencies' Sandy disaster relief internal control plans.

[a]A "partial" response for (a) indicates that the agency described its existing processes for resolving audit findings but did not specifically mention the 6-month deadline.

[b]A "partial" response for (b) indicates that the agency described its existing process for processing grantee audit reports but did not specifically mention avoiding extension requests for these reports.

[c]A "partial" response for (c) indicates that the agency described an existing, not additional, procedure to review grantee internal controls prior to funding the activity to satisfy the intent of the requirement.

Improper Payments Protocol

The Disaster Relief Act states that all programs and activities receiving funds under the act shall be deemed to be "susceptible to significant improper payments" for purposes of IPIA.[13] M-13-07 adds that all federal programs or activities receiving funds under the act are required to calculate and report an improper payment estimate. Additionally, M-13-07 notes that agencies shall manage all Sandy-related funding with the same discipline and rigor as programs that are traditionally designated as high risk for improper payments. Table 9 summarizes the requirement related to improper payments protocol.

---

[13]Pub. L. No. 107-300, 116 Stat. 2350 (Nov. 26, 2002), *codified, as amended, at* 31 U.S.C. § 3321 note.

Table 9: Adopting Improper Payments Management Protocol per M-13-07

Requirement	Required of	Exception to requirement
Agencies shall manage Sandy-related funding with the same discipline and rigor as programs traditionally designated as high risk for improper payments. All federal programs or activities receiving funds under the act are automatically considered susceptible to significant improper payments, regardless of any previous improper payment risk assessment results, and are required to calculate and report an improper payment estimate.	All programs receiving funding under the Disaster Relief Act	No exception

Source: GAO analysis of OMB Memorandum M-13-07.

As illustrated in table 10, our review of agencies' disaster relief internal control plans for all 61 programs found that agencies discussed developing a sampling methodology to produce and report an estimate of improper payments in the fiscal year 2014 reporting period for 38 programs. Agencies discussed improper payments, but did not discuss producing and reporting an estimate of improper payments for 11 programs. Agencies did not discuss improper payments for 12 programs.

Table 10: Discussion of Improper Payments Protocol in Agencies' Sandy Disaster Relief Internal Control Plans

	Number of programs			
	Total	Yes	Partial[a]	No
The agency's internal control plan discusses adopting improper payments management protocol by developing a sampling methodology consistent with current IPIA testing requirements in OMB Circular A-123 to produce and report an improper payment estimate for the fiscal year 2014 reporting period.	**61**	38	11	12

Source: GAO analysis of agencies' Sandy disaster relief internal control plans.

[a]A "partial" response indicates that the agency discussed the risk of improper payments related to the program but did not discuss producing and reporting an estimate of improper payments.

Management of Unexpended Grant Funds

The Disaster Relief Act states that funds for grants shall be expended by the grantees within the 24-month period following the agency's obligation of funds for the grant, unless OMB waives this requirement for a particular grant program and submits a written justification for such waiver to the Committees on Appropriations of the U.S. Senate and the House of Representatives. The act also states that agencies shall include a term in the grant that requires the grantee to return any funds to the agency that are not expended within this 24-month period. M-13-07 expands on the act by stating that agencies shall ensure that each proposed grant activity has clear timelines for execution and completion within the statutory period available for grantee expenditure. Table 11 summarizes the requirements related to the management of unexpended grant funds.

Table 11: Management of Unexpended Grant Funds per M-13-07

Requirement	Required of	Exception to requirement
a. All awards under the Disaster Relief Act must require grantees to expend award funds within the 24-month period following the agency's obligation of those funds.	All grant programs	Not required if agency obtains waiver from OMB
b. Each agency shall require grantees to return to the agency any funds not expended within the 24-month period following the agency's obligation of funds for the grant.		
c. Agencies shall ensure that each proposed grant activity has clear timelines for execution within and completion within the statutory period available for grantee expenditure.		
d. Each agency must ensure that any requests to waive or extend this period are limited to only those activities that are long term by design, where it is impracticable to expend funds within the 24-month period and achieve program missions.	All grant programs	Not required if agency does not plan to apply for waiver from OMB

Source: GAO analysis of OMB Memorandum M-13-07.

As illustrated in table 12, our review found that some agencies' internal control plans did not address OMB's four requirements related to the management of unexpended grant funds for all 17 grant programs. However, it is not clear whether all of these four requirements apply to each grant program because agencies may be planning to request waivers of the 24-month expenditure requirement for certain of their grant programs.

Table 12: Discussion of the Management of Unexpended Grant Funds in Agencies' Sandy Disaster Relief Internal Control Plans

The agency's internal control plan discusses the management of unexpended grant funds by:	Number of programs			
	Total	Yes	Partial	No
a. Requiring grantees to expend award funds within the 24-month period following the agency's obligation of those funds.	17	13	2[a]	2
b. Requiring grantees to return to the agency any funds not expended within the 24-month period following the agency's obligation of funds for the grant.	17	6	0	11
c. Ensuring that each proposed grant activity has clear timelines for execution within and completion within the statutory period available for grantee expenditure.	17	9	2[b]	6
d. Ensuring that any requests to OMB to waive or extend this period are limited to only those activities that are long term by design, where it is impracticable to expend funds within the 24-month period and achieve program missions.	17	9	3[c]	5

Source: GAO analysis of agencies' Sandy disaster relief internal control plans.

[a]A "partial" response for (a) indicates that the agency discussed the 24-month expenditure requirement but did not indicate that this requirement applied to all grant funds.

[b]A "partial" response for (c) indicates that the agency discussed the timely completion but did not discuss clear timelines for execution of each proposed grant activity.

[c]A "partial" response for (d) indicates that the agency discussed applying for a waiver from OMB but did not discuss how it will ensure that requests for waivers are limited to only those activities that are long term by design.

Several Weaknesses Limited the Effectiveness of OMB's Guidance in Providing Comprehensive Oversight of Sandy Disaster Funding

OMB issued guidance to provide oversight over Sandy disaster funding, which represents an important step toward accountability over these funds. Several weaknesses limited the effectiveness of this guidance in providing a comprehensive oversight mechanism for these funds. Specifically, the guidance (1) focused on the identification of incremental risks without adequate linkages to demonstrate that known risks had been adequately addressed, (2) provided agencies with significant flexibility without requirements for documentation or criteria for claiming exceptions, and (3) resulted in certain agencies' developing their internal control plans at the same time that funds needed to be quickly distributed. The demand for rapid response and recovery assistance suggests that a proactive approach is needed in providing guidance to agencies to ensure accountability over disaster relief funding, prior to a disaster occurring.

Linkage to Known Control Risks Could Help Ensure That All Risks Are Considered

The internal control plans prepared by the agencies under M-13-07 were intended to mitigate incremental risk, and therefore they did not provide comprehensive information on all known risks and internal controls that may affect the programs that received the Sandy disaster funding. For many years, we and the IG community have identified internal control weaknesses in the federal government related to agencies receiving funds for disaster assistance. For example, following Hurricane Katrina, we reported on a number of internal control weaknesses related to contracting issues, such as federal agencies involved in responding to the disaster that had inadequate acquisition plans for carrying out their assigned responsibilities, insufficient knowledge of the market or unsound ordering practices that led to excessive or wasteful expenditures, and insufficient staff available for monitoring and oversight.[14] We also identified control weaknesses related to grants management following Hurricanes Katrina and Rita,[15] such as

- determining the amount of damage that was actually disaster related;

- sharing project information among intergovernmental participants during project development, and limitations in how the status of projects is tracked; and

- inadequate human capital capacity, especially early on in the recovery.

Similarly, IGs have reported on internal control weaknesses related to accountability over disaster assistance. For example, IGs have reported that grantees did not complete their disaster relief projects in a timely manner and did not ensure the use of funds for intended purposes,[16] and that states did not provide timely reporting on activity progress related to grant funding as some activities were not reported on until the projects were complete.[17]

When we compared the incremental risks identified by the agencies receiving funds for Sandy disaster relief with risks identified in prior GAO, IG, and financial statement audit reports related to grants management,

---

[14]GAO, *Catastrophic Disasters: Enhanced Leadership, Capabilities, and Accountability Controls Will Improve the Effectiveness of the Nation's Preparedness, Response, and Recovery System*, GAO-06-618 (Washington, D.C.: Sept. 6, 2006).

[15]GAO, *Disaster Recovery: FEMA's Public Assistance Grant Program Experienced Challenges with Gulf Coast Rebuilding*, GAO-09-129 (Washington, D.C.: Dec. 18, 2008).

[16]Department of Housing and Urban Development, *Fiscal Year 2012 Agency Financial Report* (Washington, D.C.: Nov. 16, 2012).

[17]Department of Housing and Urban Development, Office of Inspector General, *State Community Development Block Grant Hurricane Disaster Recovery Program*, 2013-FW-0001 (Washington, D.C.: Mar. 28, 2013).

contract management, improper payments, and other internal control weaknesses for programs receiving Sandy funding, we determined that some of the risks in these reports were not included in the Sandy disaster relief internal control plans. For example, one agency that reported that it will expend its Sandy disaster relief funds through contracts did not identify any incremental risks. Our review of prior GAO, IG, and financial statement audit reports found significant risks related to the agency's contract management. According to *Standards for Internal Control in the Federal Government*, internal control should provide for an assessment of the risks the agency faces from both external and internal sources. Management needs to comprehensively identify risks and should consider all significant interactions between the entity and other parties as well as internal factors at both the entity-wide and activity levels. Because the internal control plans prepared by the agencies are a subset of the complete set of risks related to programs receiving Sandy disaster relief funding, they are not effective for providing comprehensive oversight of Sandy disaster relief funds.[18] A documented, comprehensive risk assessment is necessary to help to ensure that agencies have considered all risks when designing internal controls.

Specific Criteria and Justification for Significant Decisions Could Improve Guidance

As described previously, OMB guidance listed various elements of additional internal control that at a minimum should have been reflected in the agencies' internal control plans. However, the guidance included language that allowed agencies significant flexibility in deciding whether they needed to design additional internal controls. M-13-07 did not provide specific criteria for agencies to follow to claim exemptions from requirements, and the guidance did not require agencies to document their rationales for not including additional internal controls in their internal control plans. For example, M-13-07 states that agencies should conduct additional levels of review "as appropriate" and should increase monitoring and oversight of grant recipients "to the extent appropriate to mitigate risk and possible under budgetary constraints." The guidance did not provide criteria for determining "appropriateness" or "budgetary constraints." We found that some agencies did not discuss additional levels of review despite having identified incremental risk and did not

---

[18]Further, the effectiveness of the internal controls over Sandy disaster relief funding will not be known until implementation of these plans has been completed and reviewed. Various agencies' IGs have begun or are planning work to assess the implementation of controls over the Hurricane Sandy funding. In addition, the Task Force and the Recovery Board have specific oversight roles.

discuss increased monitoring and oversight of grant recipients for some of their grant programs. Because M-13-07 did not require agencies to document their reasons for these omissions, the extent to which the agencies considered the need for these additional internal controls is not apparent from the Sandy disaster relief internal control plans.

Additionally, M-13-07 required agencies to make an annual certification that the appropriate policies and controls were in place for activities and expenses related to Hurricane Sandy. M-13-07 provides agencies flexibility by stating that this annual certification for Hurricane Sandy funding "can be included" as part of the agencies' annual assurance statements. According to OMB staff, OMB expected agencies to leverage their existing annual internal control review process performed in accordance with OMB Circular A-123 to include the internal controls related to activities and expenses funded by the Disaster Relief Act related to Hurricane Sandy. However, M-13-07 did not include specific requirements linking the annual review of controls to any additional control requirements for disaster-related funding. In light of the amount of funds involved and the risks associated with the funds provided by the Disaster Relief Act, on August 2, 2013, we sent a letter to the Director of OMB requesting consideration for sending written instructions to federal agencies to ensure that agency management includes the programs receiving funds for disaster assistance for Hurricane Sandy in their annual internal control reviews and assessments for fiscal year 2013. Such linkage between the incremental risks and mitigating controls related to disaster funding and efforts to address known internal control risks would be an important factor in providing comprehensive oversight of the internal control risks for the programs receiving disaster relief funds.

Standard Guidance Could Help Ensure That Controls Are Designed Timely

In addition to the lack of comprehensive information on risks and internal controls, there is a risk that the incremental internal controls for Sandy disaster relief funding may not have been designed in time for its distribution. The Disaster Relief Act, which required OMB to issue guidance, was enacted on January 29, 2013. OMB had a short time frame to develop and issue the internal control guidance. As noted earlier, on February 19, 2013, OMB sent the Chief Financial Officer community advance notice of its impending guidance, and OMB finalized its guidance by issuing M-13-07 on March 12, 2013. In many cases, agencies developed and implemented the internal control plans at the same time that the funds needed to be quickly distributed. The Disaster Relief Act required agencies to submit their internal control plans by March 31, 2013, and agencies reported that they had already obligated approximately $4.6 billion as of that date.

The limitations we identified in implementing M-13-07 illustrate that developing comprehensive internal control plans while a disaster unfolds is not feasible, and a proactive approach could help ensure that controls are designed timely. For example, OMB has provided standard procurement guidance, through its *Emergency Acquisitions Guide*, to assist the federal contracting community with carrying out procurement activities during disasters and other emergencies.[19] As we have previously reported, following a disaster, decision makers face a tension between the demand for rapid response and recovery assistance—including assistance to victims—and implementing appropriate controls and accountability mechanisms.[20] The risk for fraud and abuse grows when billions of dollars are being spent quickly.[21] Weather-related events have cost the nation tens of billions of dollars in damages over the past decade. In our 2013 high-risk series, we reported that the United States Global Change Research Program has observed that the impacts and costliness of weather disasters will increase in significance, as what are considered "rare" events become more common and intense because of climate change.[22] We previously reported that the growing number of disaster declarations—98 in fiscal year 2011 compared with 65 in 2004—has contributed to higher federal disaster costs.[23] These impacts pose significant financial risks for the federal government, which owns extensive infrastructure, insures property through federal flood and crop insurance programs, provides technical assistance to state and local governments, and provides emergency aid in response to natural disasters. Without standard internal control guidance in place prior to future disasters, agencies may not be able to ensure that internal controls

---

[19]Office of Federal Procurement Policy, *Emergency Acquisitions Guide* (Jan. 14, 2011). The Office of Federal Procurement Policy is the entity within OMB charged with providing overall direction in procurement policy and leadership in the development of procurement systems in executive agencies.

[20]GAO-06-618.

[21]See, for example, GAO, *American Recovery and Reinvestment Act: GAO's Role in Helping to Ensure Accountability and Transparency*, GAO-09-453T (Washington, D.C.: Mar. 5, 2009), and *Hurricanes Katrina and Rita Disaster Relief: Prevention Is the Key to Minimizing Fraud, Waste, and Abuse in Recovery Efforts*, GAO-07-418T (Washington, D.C.: Jan. 29, 2007).

[22]GAO, *High-Risk Series: An Update*, GAO-13-283 (Washington, D.C.: February 2013).

[23]GAO, *Federal Disaster Assistance: Improved Criteria Needed to Assess a Jurisdiction's Capability to Respond and Recover on Its Own*, GAO-12-838 (Washington, D.C.: Sept. 12, 2012).

for disaster relief funding are effectively designed and timely implemented for all related funding.

Conclusions

When disasters occur, the destruction caused by those disasters must be addressed immediately, and disaster relief funding must be delivered expeditiously. However, the risk for fraud and abuse increases when billions of dollars are being spent quickly. Our past work and that of the IG community has shown that effective controls and comprehensive accountability mechanisms for the use of resources related to a disaster are essential to ensure that resources are used appropriately. Relying on incremental disaster relief internal control plans cannot ensure that comprehensive information on risks and related internal controls will be adequate to ensure the safeguarding of disaster funds. Although M-13-07 represents an important step in the right direction, establishing more robust internal control guidance that can be applied to future disaster relief funding would allow agencies to proactively identify risks and develop internal controls prior to receiving such funding. Further, linking the additional risks identified in incremental plans to the complete set of known risks and related internal controls can help agency management and external entities, including Congress, to provide effective oversight of the funds.

Recommendation for Executive Action

To proactively prepare for oversight of future disaster relief funding, we recommend that the Director of OMB develop standard guidance for federal agencies to use in designing internal control plans for disaster relief funding. Such guidance could leverage existing internal control review processes and should include, at a minimum, the following elements:

- robust criteria for identifying and documenting incremental risks and mitigating controls related to the funding and

- requirements for documenting the linkage between the incremental risks related to disaster funding and efforts to address known internal control risks.

Agency Comments

We requested comments on a draft of the report from the Director of the Office of Management and Budget or her designee. On November 14, 2013, staff from OMB's Office of Federal Financial Management provided oral comments and stated that they generally agreed with our recommendation and requested additional information on the findings to inform future guidance. They also provided technical comments, which we incorporated as appropriate.

We are sending copies of this report to interested congressional committees, the Director of the Office of Management and Budget, and the 19 agencies receiving funds under the Disaster Relief Act. In addition, the report is available at no charge on the GAO website at http://www.gao.gov.

If you or your staffs have any questions about this report, please contact me at (202) 512-2623 or davisbh@gao.gov. Contact points for our Offices of Congressional Relations and Public Affairs may be found on the last page of this report. GAO staff members who made key contributions to this report are listed in appendix III.

Beryl H. Davis
Director
Financial Management and Assurance

Appendix I: Objectives, Scope, and Methodology

The Disaster Relief Appropriations Act, 2013 (Disaster Relief Act),[1] mandated GAO to review the design of the internal control plans prepared by federal agencies receiving funds under the Disaster Relief Act. This report addresses the extent to which (1) the internal control plans prepared by federal agencies complied with Office of Management and Budget (OMB) guidance and (2) OMB's guidance was effective for providing comprehensive oversight of the internal control risks for the programs receiving funds for Sandy disaster relief.

To determine the extent to which the internal control plans prepared by federal agencies complied with OMB guidance, we obtained the Sandy disaster relief internal control plans for the 19 federal agencies administering the 61 programs receiving funds under the Disaster Relief Act and compared them to OMB Memorandum M-13-07 (M-13-07).[2]

To determine the extent to which OMB's guidance was effective for providing comprehensive oversight of the internal control risks for the programs receiving funds for Sandy disaster relief, we reviewed the internal control plans and M-13-07 against *Standards for Internal Control in the Federal Government.*[3] We interviewed OMB staff and agency officials regarding the development and implementation of M-13-07. In addition, we compared the agencies' identified incremental risks to prior GAO and inspector general (IG) findings associated with internal control risks for agency programs receiving funds for Sandy disaster relief. Specifically, we reviewed the following:

- GAO, *High-Risk Series: An Update*, GAO-13-283;[4]

- GAO reports and findings from 2010 to 2013 that focused on programs receiving funding under the Disaster Relief Act, and GAO work related to Hurricane Katrina or the American Recovery and Reinvestment Act of 2009;

---

[1]Pub. L. No. 113-2, 127 Stat. 4 (Jan. 29, 2013).

[2]Office of Management and Budget, *Accountability for Funds Provided by the Disaster Relief Appropriations Act*, Memorandum No. M-13-07 (Mar. 12, 2013).

[3]GAO, *Standards for Internal Control in the Federal Government*, GAO/AIMD-00-21.3.1 (Washington, D.C.: November 1999).

[4]GAO, *High-Risk Series: An Update*, GAO-13-283 (Washington, D.C.: February 2013).

GAO-14-58 Hurricane Sandy Relief

- agencies' IG reports from 2010 to 2013 that focus on programs
  receiving Disaster Relief Act funds;

- agencies' fiscal year 2012 financial statement auditor's reports,
  including reports on internal control over financial reporting and
  reported noncompliance with laws and regulations, fiscal year 2012
  reported improper payments, and management's statement of
  assurance related to 31 U.S.C. § 3512(c)-(d), commonly known as the
  Federal Managers' Financial Integrity Act, and OMB Circular No. A-
  123;[5] and

- agencies' fiscal year 2012 annual reviews of programs and
  identification of those susceptible to significant improper payments.

In addition, we obtained information from agencies regarding the status of
obligations of Sandy disaster relief funding and the impact of
sequestration on these funds. We also obtained information from agency
IGs regarding their ongoing or planned audit work related to Sandy
disaster relief funding.

We conducted this performance audit from March 2013 to November
2013 in accordance with generally accepted government auditing
standards. Those standards require that we plan and perform the audit to
obtain sufficient, appropriate evidence to provide a reasonable basis for
our findings and conclusions based on our audit objectives. We believe
that the evidence obtained provides a reasonable basis for our findings
and conclusions based on our audit objectives.

---

[5]Office of Management and Budget, *Management's Responsibility for Internal Control*,
OMB Circular No. A-123 (Washington, D.C.: Dec. 21, 2004).

Appendix II: Federal Agencies' Programs or Appropriation Accounts Receiving Supplemental Funds under the Disaster Relief Appropriations Act, 2013

Table 13 presents the federal agencies and programs or appropriation accounts receiving funding under the Disaster Relief Act. Under the authority granted by the Balanced Budget and Emergency Deficit Control Act of 1985, as amended, OMB determined that these supplemental appropriations were to be included in the fiscal year 2013 base subject to sequestration under section 251A of that act.[1] The amounts included in this report are drawn from the Disaster Relief Act as originally enacted and are not adjusted to account for sequestration.[2]

Table 13: Agencies and Programs or Appropriation Accounts Receiving Funds under the Disaster Relief Act

	Agency	Component	Program or appropriation account	Amount (not adjusted for sequestration)
1	Department of Housing and Urban Development (HUD)	Community Planning and Development	Community Development Fund	$16,000,000,000
Total HUD				**$16,000,000,000**
2	Department of Transportation (DOT)	Federal Transit Administration	Public Transportation Emergency Relief Program	$10,900,000,000
3		Federal Highway Administration	Federal-Aid Highways - Emergency Relief Program	$2,022,000,000
4		Federal Railroad Administration	Grants to the National Railroad Passenger Corporation	$86,000,000
5			Operating Subsidy Grants to the National Railroad Passenger Corporation	$32,000,000
6		Federal Aviation Administration	Facilities and Equipment (Airport and Airway Trust Fund)	$30,000,000
Total DOT				**$13,070,000,000**

[1] 2 U.S.C. § 901a. *See also* Office of Management and Budget, *OMB Report to the Congress on the Joint Committee Sequestration for Fiscal Year 2013* (Mar. 1, 2013) (*OMB Sequestration Report*), and GAO, *March 1 Joint Committee Sequestration for Fiscal Year 2013*, B-324723 (Washington, D.C.: July 31, 2013).

[2] The majority of appropriation accounts that received funding under the Disaster Relief Act were categorized as nondefense discretionary spending and therefore were subject to a reduction of 5.0 percent of their budgetary resources. Accounts that were categorized as nondefense mandatory spending were subject to a 5.1 percent reduction, and accounts that were categorized as defense discretionary spending were subject to a 7.8 percent reduction. Some accounts were exempt from sequestration as well. The actual sequestration of Disaster Relief Act funds in a program, project, or activity within an account may vary, depending on other sources of sequestrable funding in the program. *See* Office of Management and Budget, *OMB Sequestration Report.*

	Agency	Component	Program or appropriation account	Amount (not adjusted for sequestration)
7	Department of Homeland Security (DHS)	Federal Emergency Management Agency	Disaster Relief Fund	$11,487,735,000
8			Disaster Assistance Direct Loan Program Account	$300,000,000
9		Coast Guard	Acquisition, Construction, and Improvements	$274,233,000
10		Domestic Nuclear Detection Office	Systems Acquisition	$3,869,000
11		Science and Technology	Research, Development, Acquisition, and Operations	$3,249,000
12		United States Customs and Border Protection	Salaries and Expenses	$1,667,000
13		United States Immigration and Customs Enforcement	Salaries and Expenses	$855,000
14		United States Secret Service	Salaries and Expenses	$300,000
Total DHS				**$12,071,908,000**
15	Department of the Army	Corps of Engineers - Civil	Construction	$3,461,000,000
16			Flood Control and Coastal Emergencies	$1,008,000,000
17			Operation and Maintenance	$821,000,000
18			Investigations	$50,000,000
19			Expenses	$10,000,000
Total Department of Army				**$5,350,000,000**
20	Department of the Interior (DOI)		Departmental Operations, Office of the Secretary	$360,000,000
21		National Park Service	Construction	$348,000,000
22			Historic Preservation Fund	$50,000,000
23		Fish and Wildlife Service	Construction	$68,200,000
24		Bureau of Safety and Environmental Enforcement	Oil Spill Research	$3,000,000
Total DOI				**$829,200,000**
25	Small Business Administration (SBA)		Disaster Loans Program Account (including Transfer of Funds)	$520,000,000
26			Disaster Loans Program Account (merged with Salaries and Expenses)	$259,000,000
27			Salaries and Expenses	$20,000,000

	Agency	Component	Program or appropriation account	Amount (not adjusted for sequestration)
28			Office of Inspector General	$5,000,000
Total SBA				**$804,000,000**
29	Department of Health and Human Services (HHS)		Office of the Secretary, Public Health and Social Services Emergency Fund	$800,000,000
Total HHS				**$800,000,000**
30	Environmental Protection Agency (EPA)		State and Tribal Assistance Grants	$600,000,000
31			Leaking Underground Storage Tank Fund	$5,000,000
32			Hazardous Substance Superfund	$2,000,000
33			Environmental Programs and Management	$725,000
Total EPA				**$607,725,000**
34	Department of Commerce (DOC)	National Oceanic and Atmospheric Administration	Procurement, Acquisition, and Construction	$186,000,000
35			Operations, Research, and Facilities	$140,000,000
Total DOC				**$326,000,000**
36	Department of Veterans Affairs (VA)		Departmental Administration, Construction, Major Projects	$207,000,000
37			Departmental Administration, Information Technology Systems	$531,000
38		Veterans Health Administration	Medical Services	$21,000,000
39			Medical Facilities	$6,000,000
40		National Cemetery Administration	National Cemetery Administration	$2,100,000
Total VA				**$236,631,000**
41	Department of Agriculture (USDA)		Office of the Secretary, Emergency Conservation Activities	$218,000,000
42		Food and Nutrition Service	Commodity Assistance Program	$6,000,000
43		Forest Service	Capital Improvement and Maintenance	$4,400,000
Total USDA				**$228,400,000**

	Agency	Component	Program or appropriation account	Amount (not adjusted for sequestration)
44	Department of Defense (DOD)	Navy	Operation and Maintenance, Navy	$40,015,000
45		Army National Guard	Military Construction	$24,235,000[a]
46			Operation and Maintenance, Army National Guard	$3,165,000
47			Revolving and Management Funds, Defense Working Capital Funds	$24,200,000
48		Air Force	Operation and Maintenance, Air Force	$8,500,000
49		Air National Guard	Operation and Maintenance, Air National Guard	$5,775,000
50		Army	Operation and Maintenance, Army	$5,370,000
51			Procurement of Ammunition, Army	$1,310,000
Total DOD				**$112,570,000**
52	Department of Labor (DOL)	Employment and Training Administration	Training and Employment Services	$25,000,000
Total DOL				**$25,000,000**
53	Department of Justice (DOJ)	Federal Bureau of Investigation	Salaries and Expenses	$10,020,000
54		Federal Prison System	Buildings and Facilities	$10,000,000
55		Drug Enforcement Administration	Salaries and Expenses	$1,000,000
56		Bureau of Alcohol, Tobacco, Firearms, and Explosives	Salaries and Expenses	$230,000
Total DOJ				**$21,250,000**
57	National Aeronautics and Space Administration (NASA)		Construction and Environmental Compliance and Restoration	$15,000,000
Total NASA				**$15,000,000**
58	General Services Administration (GSA)		Real Property Activities, Federal Buildings Fund	$7,000,000
Total GSA				**$7,000,000**
59	Social Security Administration (SSA)		Limitation on Administrative Expenses	$2,000,000[a]
Total SSA				**$2,000,000**

	Agency	Component	Program or appropriation account	Amount (not adjusted for sequestration)
60	Smithsonian Institution		Salaries and Expenses	$2,000,000
Total Smithsonian Institution				**$2,000,000**
61	Legal Services Corporation (LSC)		Payment to the Legal Services Corporation	$1,000,000
Total LSC				**$1,000,000**
Total Amount of Appropriations				**$50,509,684,000**

Source: Pub. L. No. 113-2.

[a]The Disaster Relief Act appropriated no new funds for this account, but rather made available an additional amount of $2,000,000 to be derived from unobligated funds previously appropriated.

Appendix III: GAO Contact and Staff Acknowledgments

GAO Contact	Beryl H. Davis, (202) 512-2623 or davisbh@gao.gov
Staff Acknowledgments	In addition to the contact named above, Michael Hansen (Assistant Director), Kim McGatlin (Assistant Director), Gloria Cano, Oliver Culley, Francine DelVecchio, Gabrielle Fagan, Patrick Frey, James Healy, Wilfred Holloway, Jason Kelly, Jason Kirwan, Felicia Lopez, Andrew Seehusen, Danietta Williams, and Matthew Zaun made key contributions to this report.

GAO's Mission	The Government Accountability Office, the audit, evaluation, and investigative arm of Congress, exists to support Congress in meeting its constitutional responsibilities and to help improve the performance and accountability of the federal government for the American people. GAO examines the use of public funds; evaluates federal programs and policies; and provides analyses, recommendations, and other assistance to help Congress make informed oversight, policy, and funding decisions. GAO's commitment to good government is reflected in its core values of accountability, integrity, and reliability.
Obtaining Copies of GAO Reports and Testimony	The fastest and easiest way to obtain copies of GAO documents at no cost is through GAO's website (http://www.gao.gov). Each weekday afternoon, GAO posts on its website newly released reports, testimony, and correspondence. To have GAO e-mail you a list of newly posted products, go to http://www.gao.gov and select "E-mail Updates."
Order by Phone	The price of each GAO publication reflects GAO's actual cost of production and distribution and depends on the number of pages in the publication and whether the publication is printed in color or black and white. Pricing and ordering information is posted on GAO's website, http://www.gao.gov/ordering.htm.
	Place orders by calling (202) 512-6000, toll free (866) 801-7077, or TDD (202) 512-2537.
	Orders may be paid for using American Express, Discover Card, MasterCard, Visa, check, or money order. Call for additional information.
Connect with GAO	Connect with GAO on Facebook, Flickr, Twitter, and YouTube. Subscribe to our RSS Feeds or E-mail Updates. Listen to our Podcasts. Visit GAO on the web at www.gao.gov.
To Report Fraud, Waste, and Abuse in Federal Programs	Contact:
	Website: http://www.gao.gov/fraudnet/fraudnet.htm E-mail: fraudnet@gao.gov Automated answering system: (800) 424-5454 or (202) 512-7470
Congressional Relations	Katherine Siggerud, Managing Director, siggerudk@gao.gov, (202) 512-4400, U.S. Government Accountability Office, 441 G Street NW, Room 7125, Washington, DC 20548
Public Affairs	Chuck Young, Managing Director, youngc1@gao.gov, (202) 512-4800 U.S. Government Accountability Office, 441 G Street NW, Room 7149 Washington, DC 20548